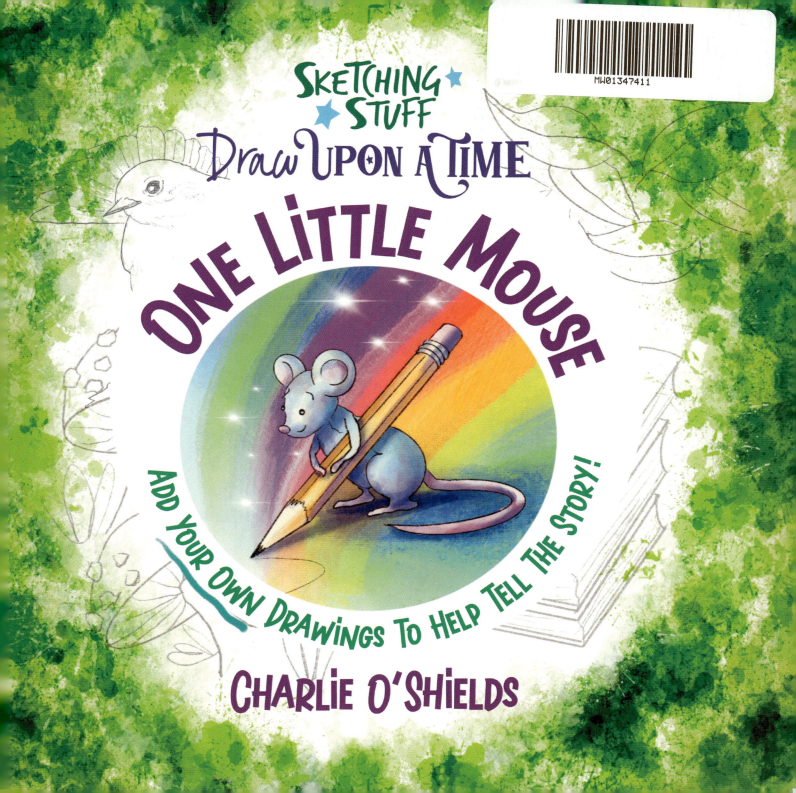

Written & Illustrated by Charlie O'Shields

doodlewash BOOKS

doodlewash.com

Copyright © 2021 Charlie O'Shields

All rights reserved. No part of this book may be reproduced in any form or by any electronic or mechanical means, including information storage and retrieval systems, without written permission from the author, except for the use of brief quotations in a book review. For more information, address: letspaint@doodlewash.com.

DOODLEWASH is a registered trademark of Storywize, LLC.
All Rights Reserved.

ISBN 978-0-9600219-5-6 (Hardcover)
ISBN 978-0-9600219-6-3 (Paperback)

Everyone Can Draw!

We were all born with the ability to make art from the moment we could first hold a crayon. We instinctively knew how to draw and color. This natural instinct to see and recreate the world around us is a rather magical thing indeed! Sort of like something you might only expect from a wizard or a magician. Well, that's exactly what YOU become whenever you doodle, sketch or draw! So, let's make some magic together!

Charlie O

Let's Begin!

Why hello there my friend! I'm so thrilled you're here!
You have magical powers that will soon become clear.
There's a mystery to solve, and some things are in doubt,
so I'll need your great talents to figure it all out.

You'll just need a wand, at the ready and extended.
A pencil, pen, or crayon, will all be quite splendid!
Are you ready? Oh good! There's a box just below.
Make some scribbles with your wand! Just give it a go!

PSSSST HINT: CHOOSE SOMETHING TO DRAW WITH THAT
DOESN'T BLEED THROUGH TO THE OTHER SIDE OF THE PAPER!

Wasn't that fun?
Yes, it's quite easy to DO!
All the skills that you need,
are right there inside you!
You see, a scribble is always
a wonderful start!
As the best magic comes
from inside your heart.

Are you pleased with the wand
that you've chosen my friend?
If you're not, try another,
and then we'll begin.

Wand At The Ready?

Oh that's great! How sublime!
Now, let's start our story
as we draw upon a time!

One Little Mouse

Once upon a time,
I was sitting on a stump.
I was deep inside the forest
when I heard a scary thump!

It gave me such a fright,
so I simply started running.
I'm just one little mouse, you see,
I have to be quite cunning.

That's how I ended up here,
and how I happened to meet you.
And how we're both now wondering
what it is that we should do.

You see, I'm also a wee bit lost,
and can't remember my way back.
So, I was hoping that you'd help me out?
Get on the proper track?

I know that we've just met,
so I don't mean to impose.
But, it's often fun to take a path,
and find out where it goes.

And you're holding a wand,
so I know you're the one.
A wizard! You must be!
This will all be quite fun!

Perhaps we could retrace my steps?
Find out where they lead?
Oh dear, I almost forgot!
There's still one thing we need.

We're not properly introduced,
and I'm certainly to blame.
Yet, I'm quite sure that if you tried,
you could GUESS MY NAME!

Indeed! That's my name!
That was really quite slick.
You're so very talented.
That was such a great trick!

We're going to get along great!
I'm so happy that we've met!
Sometimes, you simply never know
the next friend that you'll get.

Let's head back to that spot
where I was just sitting.
It's as good as any place to start.
Yes! Quite fitting!

I hope whatever made
that thump is now history.
But, together, I'm certain
we'll unravel this mystery!

Here we are. It's just here!
Yes, this is the spot!
I think it must be safe now,
or then again, perhaps not.

There's a rather large footprint
right there on the ground.
I hope whatever made that
isn't lurking around.

DRAW WHAT THE MOUSE SAW!

Of course, since I'm only
a wee little mouse,
most footprints I see
look as big as a house!

There's something lying
next to it. It could be a clue!
Why, it's my **FAVORITE FRUIT!**
But, I bet it's yours too!

My that looks so yummy!
What creature abandons food?
I wonder if it was startled too,
or just not in the mood?

Oh dear, it's all so confusing,
and I don't mean to be a grump.
I'm just so scared of losing time,
and worried about that thump.

The thump was loud,
but then again,
I have quite tiny ears.
Perhaps it wasn't much at all
to warrant all these fears.

I guess things can be frightening
whenever they are new.
Sometimes, I think it helps
to change your point of view.

Look above us there!
A Bird is sitting in that tree!
Imagine sitting so high up
and all that you might see!

I've always had a wish
that maybe one day I could fly.
But I wasn't born with wings,
so I never thought to try.

I guess it's best to use
the skills and talents you possess.
Rather than worry over missing bits
that make you feel like less.

So, I'll climb up there and see
what this bird is keeping under wraps.
Perhaps then you could use your wand
to fill in any gaps?

Draw What The Mouse Saw!

That's quite a lovely bird,
but it only just arrived.
Yet, the story I just heard,
did seem a bit contrived.

I saw a mushroom forest, though,
that's just beyond that hill.
I guess it's worth investigating,
if you're with me still?

Oh good! Let's go at once!
Just come along with me!
I think that's where
the thump came from,
so we should go and see.

I feel much more courageous
now that we are both together.
I think we're really quite prepared
for all that we might weather.

We're here my friend!
It's time to see what we can figure out.
But, I just see lots of mushrooms,
which sort of makes me doubt.

Does anything look out of place
or peculiar at all to you?
I think that I was here before,
but **SOMETHING'S MISSING**
from the view.

DRAW WHAT THE MOUSE SAW!

Oh my! You've done it again!
And jogged my memory too!
I've certainly been here before,
so that's another clue!

I was walking through this very spot,
but I didn't really look.
You see I stopped for just a moment,
and got caught up in a book.

Well, not the book, of course,
but the story was quite engaging.
If you look right there, I bet you'll find
the book that I was paging.

A stack of little books
was sitting in that very spot.
I guess left by another mouse.
I thought I might get caught!

But I never saw
another mouse.
I was all alone.
Though when I read,
I must admit,
I often tend to zone.

It was my **FAVORITE BOOK**, you see,
so I had to read it through.
Go on then! Check it out!
I'm sure you've read it too!

DRAW WHAT THE MOUSE SAW!

Yes! That's the very one!
What a wonderful tale indeed!
There's really nothing better
than a moment just to read.

I remember a rustle of leaves
that suddenly made me jump.
That's when I moved on farther,
and sat upon that stump.

So this path here must be the one
I took to this very spot!
I'm sure that it will lead me home,
and now, feel silly I forgot.

It's just that the littlest things
will often give me such a fright.
Rather than what will truly happen,
I worry about what might.

Let's head on!
I'm sure we're on the right path now!
There's a fence just up ahead,
and what appears to be a cow.

I would normally avoid things so large,
but I'm feeling rather good.
Feels a bit like courage,
doing things I thought I never would.

We've reached the fence!
And now, I see a brand new trail!
But look! There's another footprint there,
just below that rail!

Was I truly being chased by something
with such enormous feet?
Oh dear, that's not at all a creature
I would like to meet!

There's something rather odd,
that I now can't quite explain.
Something that's been sort of
weighing on my little brain.

If that creature is still out here,
then where could it be now?
Do you maybe think the thump,
was perhaps caused by that cow?

No, that's silly.
That cow has
barely moved an inch.
It's definitely the creature
with those prints
that made me flinch!

I'm getting rather hungry, though,
Since, I didn't eat any lunch.
I guess we could take a tiny break,
and then work out my hunch?

Look! There's a little picnic basket
that's sitting over there.
I'm sure whoever left it,
would surely want to share!

It doesn't appear to be something
that someone wants to hide.
I think that we should take a peek,
and find out WHAT'S INSIDE?

DRAW WHAT THE MOUSE SAW!

Wow, that all looks so wonderful,
but it's not really ours to eat.
I guess we should simply venture on,
and hope for another treat.

I would never, of course, take anything
that didn't belong to me.
But, sometimes my curiosity
makes me simply want to see!

Like that tree right there!
The one that looks so pretty.
But some leaves
seem to be missing,
which is truly quite a pity.

Do you think that you could do
that magic thing you do?
Perhaps add back some LEAVES,
at least just one or two?

DRAW WHAT THE MOUSE SAW!

That's really quite amazing!
I think you should put on a show!
You have such natural talent,
though I'm sure you already know.

I remember that tree now,
thanks to you!
This must be the way!
In fact, I think we're getting
rather close, I'd have to say!

Here's a barn! I've been here before,
but something isn't right.
I used to wave to another mouse,
when I'd pass by each night.

I would usually never ask you
to perform again so soon.
But, I'm hoping you could put that Mouse
back there below the moon?

DRAW WHAT THE MOUSE SAW!

That's the one! Why hello there!
And my memory is growing clearer!
Yes, I'm practically back home now.
Each step draws us nearer.

Though I have to say,
I'm truly enjoying
the time I've spent with you.
It's perfectly lovely, really,
something unexpected, nice and new.

I've always been a little shy
and scared to try new things.
Sometimes, I wish that I could know
just what the future brings.

Yet, now you're here with me,
and that's not something I expected.
Though still I feel that through all this,
we're growing quite connected.

But, it's getting dark,
and we should really venture on.
While other mice seem to love the night,
I far prefer the dawn.

I've always felt a wee bit different,
everywhere I go.
But I think it's great to be unique!
I'm the only me I know!

The path ahead is certainly dim.
I don't recall this part.
I'm sure I would have chosen
a much brighter place to start.

Oh look! There's a lantern
that seems to be missing its light.
Would you be so kind as to Add A Bulb
and brighten up the night?

DRAW WHAT THE MOUSE SAW!

Oh my! You did it once more!
You really never fail to amaze!
It's clever how you use that wand
in the most remarkable of ways.

The path is lit, so let's move on,
and find out where we're at.
Oh dear, my luck is running out!
Is that the world's largest cat?!

It's coming right for me!
I'm truly so sorry, but I really have to run.
You see I don't get on well with cats,
and if I stay it won't be fun.

I can't tell if the beast is hungry
or just really wants to play.
I'm not sure, in any case,
it ends well for me either way.

I think I can find a place to hide
if I can get back to that barn door.
It seems many miles away now, though!
Oh my! Did that cat just ROAR?!

Why on earth should any creature
need such terrifying fangs?!
And it's getting closer to me now!
My heart doesn't beat, it bangs!

My friend if you can still hear me,
then you can help me in this plight!
If you can use your wand again
and think of something bright!

I've no ideas to share this time,
it could be this or that.
But, please think of **Something Quick**
to distract that monster cat!

Draw Something Quick!

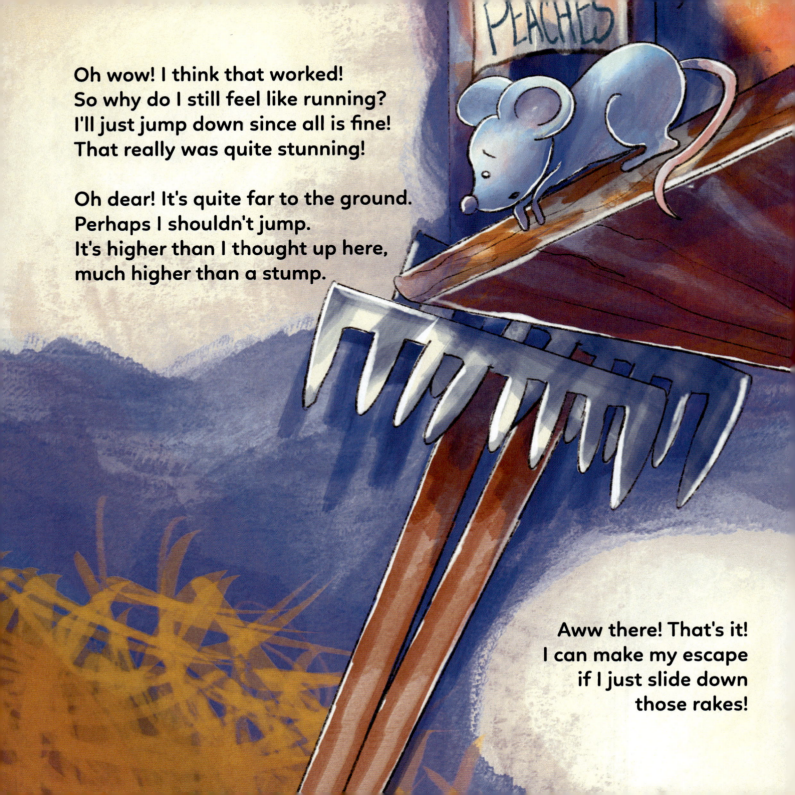

Oh wow! I think that worked!
So why do I still feel like running?
I'll just jump down since all is fine!
That really was quite stunning!

Oh dear! It's quite far to the ground.
Perhaps I shouldn't jump.
It's higher than I thought up here,
much higher than a stump.

Aww there! That's it!
I can make my escape
if I just slide down
those rakes!

It really is quite dark in here,
and there's barely any light.
There's a bit of glow
from the moon above,
but it isn't very bright.

Where am I now?
And where are you?
Oh no! This can't be the end!
I've messed things up quite utterly,
and now I've lost my friend.

I'm trapped and all alone again,
with no one who can lend a hand.
This really shouldn't be my story,
but this is always where I land.

Perhaps I wasn't ever really
meant to find my way back home.
Who would think
that one scared mouse
could do much more than roam.

I thought things might
be different now,
that I was someone new.
Yet, after all that's happened,
I'm no longer sure that's true.

I have no special magician's powers,
or a talent for creation.
But, surely with just a little hope,
I could solve my situation!

Wait! I see something over there
that looks like something from before!
Yes, it's a wand!
Just waiting there!
Just waiting on the floor!

I don't have any wizardry,
not like I've seen my friend display.
But, I can still make magic happen!
Right now! In my own way!

Oh dear! This wand is rather huge,
but I'll simply have to try.
I've totally run out of options here.
This is no time to be shy!

Alright then! I can do this,
even if I've not been here before.
I'm rather sure that every room
must surely have a door.

That worked! I'm free!
And I can see you!
Still standing by the light!
I can't believe you waited for me,
after I ran off in such a fright.

I guess you really are my friend!
Faithful, kind and true!
I'm not quite sure a mouse like me
deserves someone like you.

I tried just what you taught me
and I really made it work!
Though I do admit I lack your skills,
I bet that you would smirk.

Yet, no! You're smiling proudly now,
which makes me smile too!
It really feels quite good to know,
when someone believes in you.

There's just a few more steps to go,
and I'll be safely in my house.
And yet, I think that when I'm back,
I'll be a very different mouse.

I live just over there.
Would you like to walk me to my door?
I know our time is fleeting,
but I'd love just a minute more.

This is it!
I know it doesn't seem like much,
but it's lovely in the fall.
I would certainly
invite you in, of course,
but I fear it's a bit too small.

What's that I heard you say?
You'd like to
Draw Something Just For Me?
Oh wow! I'd love that very much.
I just can't wait to see!

Draw Something For The Mouse!

Why that's just brilliant!
I'll cherish it every single day!
It's a beautiful reminder of the one
I met along the way.

Well, I guess I should go back inside.
It's getting rather late.
Yet, I've just spotted something odd,
that we really must set straight.

You're standing on another of those
footprints strewn around.
Well, not so much on as in,
right there upon the ground.

That's rather strange indeed,
and not what I thought I knew.
Don't you find it odd the footprint fits
exactly with your shoe?

Wait! If that's the case,
then the thump
that started this all,
wasn't caused
by something scary,
just someone rather tall.

It was **YOU!**
who made that sound I heard,
the one that made me run.
But then we found each other,
and now our story
is almost done.

Well, I guess that solves
this mystery,
and I learned a thing or two.
I was a bit too quick to run,
but so thrilled I ran into you.

I guess I've learned to
take things slower,
not jumping to critique.
That everything big isn't scary,
and everything small isn't weak.

I think in the end,
my biggest hope
is to be a bit more like you.
I don't mean
quite so tall, of course,
but perhaps an **ARTIST**, too.

DRAW WHAT THE MOUSE IMAGINED!

You've shown me
that a simple wand
can do so many things.
Drawing out all the best in life
and the beauty that it brings.

I guess I'll say goodbye for now,
but I don't think this is the end.
Someday, there'll be another mystery
that simply needs a friend.

I hope you'll keep on making magic,
each and every day.
I'm sure that there are many others
you will help along the way.